Co-Conspirators: Artist and Collector
The Collection of James Cottrell and Joseph Lovett

at the Orlando Museum of Art

July 24 – October 31, 2004

Exhibition Curated by:

Sue Scott

Essays by:

Raphael Rubinstein

Sue Scott

Printed in the United States

ISBN# 1-880699-07-9

Library of Congress Catalog Card Number: 200409558

Cover: Residence of James Cottrell and Joseph Lovett

Accredited by the American Association of Museums, the Orlando Museum of Art is supported by earned income, the Council of 101, donations from individuals, corporations and foundations, and sponsored in part by United Arts of Central Florida with funds from the United Arts campaign, State of Florida, Department of State, Division of Cultural Affairs and the Florida Arts Council, and the National Endowment for the Arts.

CONTENTS

FOREWORD

The relationship between the Orlando Museum of Art (OMA) and James Cottrell and Joseph Lovett began in 2001 when they lent *tips #3 (between the lines)*, 1997-99, a large work on paper by Suzanne McClelland, for her exhibition titled *Enough Enough*. They later placed this work on long-term loan at the OMA. Also in 2001, our guest curator Sue Scott, writing for *Art & Antiques*, named them to the "Top 100 Collectors" list.

Cottrell and Lovett have assembled a unique and internationally important collection. The idea for this exhibition began when Cottrell and Lovett were thinking about renovating their home. Fortunately for the OMA, we are able to feature their outstanding collection during the renovation. We are profoundly grateful to them for sharing their art treasures for this exhibition.

Marena Grant Morrisey
Executive Director

ACKNOWLEDGMENTS

Jim Cottrell called me several years ago to tell me he and Joe Lovett were planning to renovate their home. Having previously lent work to the Orlando Museum of Art (OMA), Jim asked me if the OMA might be interested in taking their collection on long-term loan. I had known Jim and Joe several years and had heard of their collection some time before that. From the first moment I saw the collection, I was struck by its visual harmony and conceptual originality. A few years later, as part of the writing team for *Art & Antiques'* issue of America's "Top 100 Collectors," I included the Cottrell-Lovett collection in the list. So, when this opportunity arose, I jumped at the chance to bring this exceptional collection to Orlando. The result is this exhibition, *Co-Conspirators: Artist and Collector, The Collection of James Cottrell and Joseph Lovett.*

The energy and synergy that define the collecting habits of these two men also marked our collaboration. I want to thank both Jim and Joe for being so enjoyable to work with and for expanding my awareness of the international painting scene. I am also thankful to Deborah Kass, Roland Flexner, Barton Benes, Jonathan Lasker, Suzanne McClelland and Malcolm Morley for their observations and memories. I particularly want to thank Raphael Rubinstein, a senior editor at *Art in America* and known fan of painting, for his insightful and thorough essay on the artists in the show. I want to thank Meredy Jenkins for designing a beautiful catalogue, Michelle Ghorbanian for editing and Kirsty Martinsen for her assistance with copyright approval. I appreciate the work of Mauri Palmio who managed the documenting, packing and moving of the collection, Mary Barone, archivist of the collection and Roland Flexner for proofreading the copy and checklist.

As usual, the staff at the Orlando Museum of Art worked enthusiastically to bring this exhibition together. I especially appreciate the tireless efforts of Andrea Long, registrar, Kevin Boylan, preparator, Kendle Arribas, marketing coordinator, Hansen Mulford, curator and Susan Rosoff, curator of education, for their assistance on this project.

Sue Scott
Guest Curator

Jean-Michel Basquiat, *Claudio*, n.d.

CO-CONSPIRATORS: ARTIST AND COLLECTOR
THE MAKING OF A COLLECTION
By Sue Scott

In late May 2004, Jim Cottrell and I visited Malcolm Morley and his wife Lida at his studio in Brookhaven, Long Island. I had a specific project to discuss with Morley, and Jim came along to catch up with a favorite artist. Morley greeted us at the door of his home, a converted church located at the edge of town. On our way into the studio, we passed a beautiful antique cabinet packed with the objects and models found in Morley's paintings: tin soldiers, wooden boats, castles, knights and countless "three-dimensional watercolors" of ships and planes, hand-constructed from watercolor paper and then meticulously painted, often in a trompe l'oeil fashion. One of the larger models, the historic "Santa Maria," is a primary image in Morley's painting *Santa Maria with Sopwith Camel Wing* (1996), in the Cottrell-Lovett collection.

Malcolm Morley (left) with Jim Cottrell

Jim and I descended upon every inch of the studio, and the next two hours were marked by energetic exchanges as Morley showed us current paintings, new prints and pictures of previous work we had never seen. In mid-afternoon, we finally broke for lunch at a local restaurant, and then returned to the studio where inevitably Jim, the obsessive collector, purchased two of the prints we'd seen earlier. As Lida and I made some arrangements in the other room, Jim, who is an anesthesiologist, discussed science and the brain with the artist, interests they had shared over the many years they had known each other.

That same day, Joe Lovett flew to Buffalo, New York, for the closing of the exhibition *The Domain of Perfect Affection*, featuring the work of Patricia Cronin, an artist and good friend of the collectors. Joe, a film director and producer, attended the show at the University of Buffalo to film an episode for "Gallery," a subscription series for Voom, which is a high-definition cable service. The previous weekend, Jim, Joe and I visited Deborah Kass in her studio in Brooklyn to film an episode for the same series. Jim and Joe collect Kass' work in-depth and along with interviewing the artist, Joe wanted to film Jim's reaction to Kass' newest series of word paintings, which she'd been working on for several years.

I relay these three vignettes because I believe they exemplify Jim and Joe's approach to collecting art. They possess an obsessive desire to see and know everything about the artist they are interested in and after making that connection, to provide ongoing support. "Once I find someone I really like," Jim says, "I continue to acquire their work. Many of the artists we met and whose work I bought in the seventies and eighties, we still collect." [1]

Both men believe it is important to look at many works by the same artist, to read about the artists and to talk with them, if possible. Their mantra on collecting is: Learn as much as you can, in any way possible. Over the nearly 30 years they have been collecting, they have not only become friendly with a number of artists and developed deep friendships with others, they have created a life in art that occupies most of their waking hours outside of work.

In reflecting on how the collection began, Joe notes, "The work I originally collected was given to me by artist friends. I never had a desire to own grand or expensive works. I am just as happy to see art in a museum as on my own walls. But one day, Jim said to me, 'If we don't buy it, how will the artist survive?' " [2]

In a world where an artist's income can be drastically affected from year to year by the whims of fashion, patronage is an essential, but less obvious, role played by collectors such as Jim and Joe. Artist Barton Benes, whom Joe has known since 1966, concurs. "Jim and Joe buy seriously and regularly. And as my work changes or I move in new directions, they grow with me. They're willing to take the leap and go to this new place with me. They've stuck with me, always. They're true." [3] Over the years, Benes has made works using currency and about AIDS. He has also created "mini-museums" that deal with topics such as murder

Manuel Neri, *Seated Female Figure*, 1961

or food. And, in the final stages of production is a film on Benes' art titled "No Secrets," which Joe is producing.

The two collectors do not often commission works, but several years ago they commissioned Donald Baechler to make a fountain for their backyard (pictured on back of catalogue). Although sculpture is not a focal point of their collection, another fine example is *Seated Female Figure* (1961) by Manuel Neri, which has the same expressive qualities and tactile surfaces that defines the aesthetic of the collectors.

Jim and Joe's approach to collecting differs from other collectors in many ways. Some collectors prefer not to meet the artist, believing the painting or object must stand on its own. Others collect one example from many artists. Some chase trends or "update" their collection over the years to reflect the changing times or their changing taste. For Jim and Joe, collecting art is a continuum linked together by experience and friendship. Today their collection numbers nearly 400 pieces and includes works by many major international artists.

Joe readily admits that for the most part collecting art is essentially Jim's passion. And he hasn't always loved the direction it's taken. In fact, he told me a few friends refer to it as the "in-spite-of-Joe" collection. "Sometimes, Jim brings home something I really don't like," he says, "but he never brings home anything that is dull. It is all work you can continue to engage with. They all have stories. I know some people move paintings around because they are bored with them. That is never the case with us. Jim moves them to allow us to see one that has been in storage." [4]

This is a collection that starts with, and is sustained by, the act of looking. "The image, or composition, has to attract me," says Jim, "but after that initial jolt of energy, you have to go somewhere with it. That is when it becomes important to understand what the artists are about, the journey they are on and what they are doing with their lives. But the image has to be there first. I have to like what I'm looking at." [5]

An offshoot of being involved in the lives of the artists one collects is the influence those artists inevitably have on that collection. This is the case with Roland Flexner, an artist represented in-depth in the Cottrell-Lovett collection, and the person responsible for introducing Jim and Joe to much of the art and many of the artists in their collection. Flexner and Jim met in 1982 through Flexner's wife Sue Williams, a film producer with whom Joe worked. After Jim's first visit to Flexner's studio, he purchased the large painting *Untitled (standing figure throwing light)* (1985).

"I thought it was very mysterious," Jim says, "and the technique was incredible. The more I learned about Flexner's unique blending of oil painting and gilding on canvas, the more I was intrigued." [6] Jim continues to collect many of Flexner's works, including numerous large paintings and several drawings. Initially, he was attracted by the exotic flavor of the work and knowing Flexner was from Nice, he associated the rich color and flatness of the paintings with the work of Henri Matisse. As with many of the artists whom Jim befriends, the two quickly found other, non-art-related points of connection. For instance, Flexner's uncle (a composite model for the flame thrower) wrote the *Flexner Report*, which served as a basis for curriculum reform for medical schools in the 1800s, and happens to be a report with which Jim is familiar.

At Flexner's studio in New York, Jim and Joe met a number of French artists. They became friendly with Edouard Prulhière when he lived in New York, painting and working as a gallery assistant to Julian Schnabel. And they became acquainted with many of the French artists who showed with Flexner and Prulhière in Paris at Galerie Meteo. Several years later, Jim and Joe visited the Flexners in Nice, a summer visit they have repeated over the years. They often spent time there visiting other artists in their studios. During their stays, they became more familiar with the School of Nice, a loosely defined "school" of three generations of artists, beginning with Yves Klein and including in its second

Roland Flexner, *Untitled (bubble drawing, FP13)*, 2002

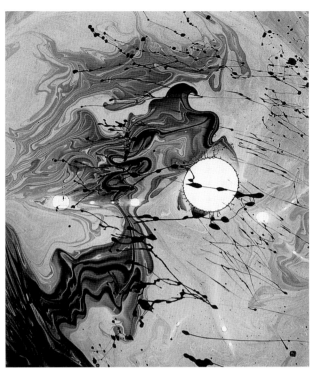

generation Noël Dolla, Daniel Dezeuze and Flexner. Through Dolla, Jim and Joe met and collected work by two of his students, Dominique Figarella and Philippe Mayaux.

During a studio visit with Flexner and Jim, I pointed out that Flexner's work, with its flat space and rich but thinly applied paint, was incongruous with much of the other work in the Cottrell-Lovett collection, which is defined by tactile, textured surfaces, bright and aggressively blended colors and abstract imagery. But as Flexner countered, "Jim, like everybody else, has contradictory approaches. I often notice he likes the medium and the material. He's attracted to relief and texture, but not necessarily the volume of the texture. He likes the refinement of the texture. What I do is extremely thin and flat and he likes that, too." [7]

Flexner does not differentiate between figuration and abstraction in his work. For example, he sees *Untitled (blue room with curving line)* (1987), with its minimalist/color field sensibility, as similar to *Untitled (people with torches)* (1986). Though Flexner does not necessarily view his work as narrative, the two works do document an "event." *Untitled (people with torches)* was not made to tell a specific story but over the years Flexner realized it could relate to his memories of religious processions in France, while the "event" in *Untitled (blue room with curving line)* is more subtle, relating to the way the paint is applied, how light reflects in a painting and how a simple, improvised line is made with a single gesture.

"It is an 'event' in the sense of Chinese calligraphy," explains Flexner. "Doing something in one breath. You start a line and end up when the breath is finished." [8] (It's interesting to note that Flexner's bubble drawings, made with soap, glycerine and India ink, are also the result of a single, extended breath.)

Not all of the connections made through Flexner were with the French community. For many years, Flexner and Malcolm Morley lived in the same apartment building on Spring Street in New York City, and Flexner introduced Morley to Jim and Joe. Their first purchase of Morley's work was a small watercolor, *Untitled (n.d.),* and they have since acquired, in addition to the painting *Santa Maria with Sopwith Camel Wing* (1996), *Still Life with Two Planes* (2001-2002) and *A Hun Burst into Flames and Another Came Spinning Earthward* (1992). Coincidentally, the latter work is the watercolor study for the large Morley painting, *Dawn Patrol* (1992), in the Orlando Museum of Art's permanent collection.

When Jim saw the paintings of Miguel Barceló exhibited at Leo Castelli Gallery in 1987, he responded immediately. After discussing the work with Flexner, who was equally enthusiastic, he purchased *In Vitro* (1987) from the exhibition. Jim was fascinated by Barceló's expressive process, his use of organic material and imagery abstracted from nature. It comes as no surprise that Jim eventually met Barceló and bought more of his work.

During a visit to Barceló's studio several years later, Jim saw four large-scale paintings that had been commissioned by the contemporary art museum in Barcelona. He loved the work, but all four paintings were spoken for. However, several months later, Barceló called him to say the museum only wanted two of the four. Was Jim interested in purchasing the other two? That is how *Soupe d'Ane* (1997), a major Barceló work, came into the Cottrell-Lovett collection.

Even as his relationships with artists develop, Jim won't let a friendship or acquaintance override his decision to acquire or not acquire a work. Flexner's *Untitled (blue room with curving line)* (1987) is a prime example of this philosophy. "I'd seen the work a lot and I wasn't interested. But Joe really loved it and encouraged me to take a second look. The more I looked, the more I saw the contrast between the two paintings (*people with torches* and *blue room with curving line*). Though they evoked different emotions and different feelings, I began to see them as a pair." [9]

Todd Murphy, *Untitled (Two Figures)*, 1994

In the early 1980s, Jim met a young, relatively unknown artist named Jean-Michel Basquiat and subsequently bought his work, which he loved for its spontaneity. Though many of Jim's friends questioned his sanity for buying Basquiat in those early days, it is a testament to his insight that these works have grown in importance. Jim believes there is a message in the work that is accessible to everyone. During one of their conversations, Basquiat told Jim that *The Three Delegates* (1982), with its brown, gold and white faces, came from the artist's memories of visiting the United Nations as a young child. Years later, *Untitled* (1994), by Todd Murphy, was acquired. Many of the qualities in this work — a raw expressiveness and a graffiti-like delivery — that attracted Jim early on to Basquiat still speak to the collector today.

The relationship between collector and artist can be a symbiotic give-and-take. Such is the case with Suzanne McClelland, whose scope of work in the Cottrell-Lovett collection spans a decade. McClelland often deals with language in her work, collecting words by listening and translating this sound and speech into visual form. The physicality of speech can be displayed in paint because paint is so flexible and malleable. And because speech comes from the brain faster than written language, abstraction is the perfect vehicle for found speech. Mystery, hidden meaning and varied interpretations — all qualities that can be found in much of the work in this collection — are attributes of art that appeal to both Jim and Joe. As McClelland notes, "Collecting spoken words is a subjective process. Collecting art is, too." [10]

Collecting McClelland's work is an indication of Jim and Joe's ongoing curiosity about art and their willingness to buy work that is not transparent. "The personal nature of Suzanne's work is not clear to me as yet," Jim wrote recently, "but as I know more of her, I'm sure it will become that way." [11]

When I asked McClelland what it meant to an artist to have the ongoing support of specific collectors, she replied:

The real collector, the kind who collects in depth and spends time with the work, has an eye that interests me. Making work is something that artists do regardless of the collector. But an artwork has a new life when it finds a home with people who follow a particular artist and put it into a context with other artists who may also reflect their thoughts and taste.

Joe Lovett (left) with Deborah Kass

It gives it a specific place in history. If I were to keep paintings to myself it could be suffocating, like home schooling – isolating and self-protective. I like to lose control of the work through somebody else's eye, and some of my paintings have been fortunate enough to end up with Jim and Joe. [12]

Deborah Kass met Jim and Joe through mutual friends. A rocky start caused by reciprocal dislike of one another's dog transformed into a close friendship and eventually into a collector/artist relationship. "I love people like Jim and Joe who want to get into my brain, to that extent," Kass says. "That and a curator or writer doing the same are things any artist wants." [13]

Over the years, Jim and Joe have bought excellent examples from each of Kass' series. They own particularly strong examples from her art history series such as, *How Do I Look?* (1991), which references Picasso; *Call of the Wild (for Pat Steir)* (1989), which quotes from Steir and uses the abstract marks of Lee Krasner; and *Short Stories* (1989), a transitional work that led to the art history painting series. "Jim and Joe own some of my best work," Kass says, "and I feel it's safe with them, in every way." [14]

David Hockney, *My Bonnie Lies Over the Sea*, 1961

"The historical references in Debbie's work made me pay more attention to contemporary painters," says Joe. "I didn't know painters that well except for French artists. Her work made me look and think about contemporary art more." [15]

David Hockney is a bit of a wild card whose work came into the collection when two of Jim and Joe's friends, Mark Berger (a schoolmate of Hockney's in London) and Nathan Kolodner (whom Jim met at the gym), introduced them to the artist and his work. The collection contains an important early painting from 1964, *Untitled (Landscape #1 and #2)*, and a large grouping of drawings used as studies for later paintings. "We liked Hockney's early imagery, or lack thereof —

images that suggest there's more to come," Jim says. "His work has hidden meanings and yet is personal." [16]

Jim met Jonathan Lasker more than a decade ago, when Lasker had his first opening at Sperone Westwater Gallery in New York. Though Jim and Joe are friendly with many artists, they also have close friendships with dealers such as David Leiber, a partner at Sperone Westwater, who introduced them to Lasker. Though Jim did not

O. Winston Link
At the Drive-In, ca. 1955

initially respond to the work, he came to appreciate the tactile quality of Lasker's paint application and purchased *Improved Expressions* (1991), from this first show. Later, he bought *Symbolic Farming* (2001), a painting he was attracted to not only for its beautiful surfaces and abstract markings, but also because it conjured up memories of his childhood in the farmland of West Virginia. (This sense of association triggered through memory or conceptual connection is another important but less obvious component of Jim and Joe's selection process. For instance, *At the Drive-In* (ca. 1955), by O. Winston Link, is a photograph of a drive-in Jim frequented as a teenager in West Virginia.)

"I have a body of work that spans about 25 years," Lasker says, "and I do like it if people collect from the different periods. It shows an engagement and dialogue with the work. I like what Jim and Joe collect. They have a strong sensibility, particularly in regard to painting. It helps if your work hangs with other artists who you feel an engagement with. It means there is a sensitivity." [17]

Taking a collection out of a domestic situation and hanging it together on the walls of a museum is a true test of whether this sensitivity exists or not. The eye and intent of the collector is revealed. We can only imagine what will happen with the Cottrell-Lovett collection when it returns home. Years ago, when I was working on an exhibition with Alex Katz, he told me his retrospective at the Whitney Museum of American Art triggered his own reassessment of his work. Many artists, I think, have that response. I believe we're seeing the Cottrell-Lovett collection at its mid-point, and that it will continue to grow and deepen. Neither Joe nor Jim has any plans to quit collecting. In fact, quite to the contrary, they recently acquired a large drawing by Jorge Queiroz, a young Portuguese artist about whom they knew nothing. But when they saw his work at Galerie Nathalie Obadia in Paris, they simply had to have it.

Collecting continues to be an obsession. And how can it be otherwise? "When I see a painting I really love, the image stays in my mind, it persists," Jim explains. "Whether I buy it or not, it haunts me." [18]

Endnotes
1. Videotaped interview with Jim Cottrell, June 2003.
2. Conversation with Joe Lovett and Jim Cottrell, January 2004.
3. Telephone interview with Barton Benes by the author, June 16, 2004.
4. E-mail from Joe Lovett to the author, June 21, 2004.
5. Ibid, videotape.
6. Conversation among Jim Cottrell, Roland Flexner and the author in Flexner's studio, April 15, 2004.
7. Ibid.
8. Ibid.
9. Ibid.
10. Conversation with Suzanne McClelland, June 20, 2004.
11. E-mail from Jim Cottrell to the author, June 13, 2004.
12. E-mail and conversation between Suzanne McClelland and the author, June 14, 2004.
13. Telephone interview with Deborah Kass by the author, June 17, 2004.
14. Ibid.
15. Conversation between Deborah Kass, Joe Lovett, Jim Cottrell and the author, June 2004.
16. Ibid, Cottrell e-mail.
17. Telephone interview with Jonathan Lasker by the author, June 17, 2004.
18. Ibid, videotape.

Jorge Queiroz, *Untitled*, 2004

INDEPENDENT AND INTERNATIONAL:
HIGHLIGHTS OF THE COTTRELL-LOVETT COLLECTION

By Raphael Rubinstein

Since I first met James Cottrell and Joe Lovett, about 10 years ago, I have been a great admirer of their art collection. A large part of this admiration has to do with aesthetic affinity: their collection includes many of my favorite artists, figures whom I've written about repeatedly. But equally important, for me, is the independence of their choices. One of the most unfortunate aspects of the booming art market of the last few decades has been the herd mentality that seems to drive most American collectors. Nearly every one of them seems to want exactly the same artists, which not only drives up prices (good for a few artists and dealers, I suppose), but also results in the same collection being cloned throughout the country. (I'm putting the stress on American collectors because this tendency seems much more pronounced here than in, say, Europe, where collections tend to be more individualistic.) Whatever the causes of this development, it seems to me not a good thing for the health of contemporary art or for culture in general.

It's safe to say that there is no collection of contemporary art in the United States like this one. Although Cottrell and Lovett have sought out works by some of the most celebrated and collected artists of the last 20 years — figures such as Jean-Michel Basquiat, David Hockney and Robert Mapplethorpe — they have also explored areas of artistic creation that few, if any, other American collectors know exist. I'm thinking in particular of the contemporary French artists (Noël Dolla, Roland Flexner, Daniel Dezeuze and others) who have such a prominent presence in the Cottrell-Lovett collection. Clearly, this is an assembly of art that follows the sensibilities of two individuals and not any critical orthodoxy or fashionable shopping list, which is what makes it so rewarding to look at and to think about. May its independent character be an inspiration to other art lovers.

Herewith, then, is some commentary on highlights of the collection.

The 1980s were marked by a return to painting. This revival, which came after a period in which conceptual and performance art seemed to dominate, was widespread, occurring throughout Europe, Latin America and the United States. It was especially strong in New York, where in the early part of the decade it was often closely involved with the burgeoning hip-hop culture and the artistic ferment of downtown Manhattan. Included in the Cottrell-Lovett collection are works by three artists who drew inspiration from, and significantly contributed to, this milieu: Jean-Michel Basquiat, Keith Haring and Donald Baechler.

Basquiat's *Three Delegates* (1982) dates from the period that Richard Marshall identifies as the earliest phase of the artist's career. "From 1980 to late 1982," says Marshall, who curated the 1992 Basquiat retrospective at the Whitney Museum of American Art, "Basquiat used painterly gestures on canvases, most often depicting skeletal figures and masklike faces that signal his obsession with mortality, and imagery derived from his street existence, such as automobiles, buildings, police, children's sidewalk games and graffiti." [1] In this painting, which combines acrylic, oil stick and collage, the trio of faces and surrounding calligraphic marks reflects two of Basquiat's biggest influences, Jean Dubuffet and Cy Twombly. What is especially striking about this painting, however, is the absence of text (the collection's other Basquiat, from two years later, *Untitled*, 1984, displays the artist's poetic use of found writing). It's one of the relatively few Basquiats from this period, which poet Rene Ricard characterized as "the happiest time" of the artist's life, which relies almost exclusively on pictorial means to convey its vision of urban pressure and anguished, totemic visages.

Keith Haring, a close friend of Basquiat's who similarly first gained fame as a graffiti artist, is represented by a rare early work. This nearly 10-foot-high untitled work dates from 1978, the year that Haring came to New York from Pennsylvania as a scholarship student at the School for Visual Arts (SVA). It was at SVA that year that Haring developed his distinctive style. As he later recalled,

"I bought a roll of oak-tag paper and cut it up and put it all over the floor and worked on this whole group of drawings. The first few were abstracts, but then these images started coming. They were humans and animals in different combinations. Then flying saucers were zapping the humans. I remember trying to figure out where this stuff came from, but I have no idea. It just grew into this group of drawings." [2] What's exciting about this work is that one can see Haring, in these rhythmic sequences of dashes, dots and curves, on the verge of discovering the pictographic vocabulary that would soon be disseminated around the world.

While Haring was at SVA, a dozen blocks away another young painter, Donald Baechler, was studying at Cooper Union. Although he initially showed at the same gallery (Tony Shafrazi Gallery) as Haring and favored a raw, intentionally primitive figuration, Baechler's work is far more involved in traditional painterly issues. Often using found figure drawings, he juxtaposes objects and figures according to an oblique but graphically potent logic, as seen in the untitled 1988 painting in the Cottrell-Lovett collection. In a 2000 interview in *Bomb* magazine, Baechler spoke about the subjects of his work. "I think that, for me, the head is almost always a kind of surrogate for a self portrait, and the flowers almost a replacement for the human figure in the paint-ing. I've made an almost intentional point of not studying botany or not learning what these flowers are that I'm drawing. I buy flowers at the Korean deli on the corner, but you know, I can barely distinguish between a tulip and a rose, which sounds stupid, but it's true. For me a flower has this very convenient, almost human dimension, with the head and the stem and the leaves replacing certain body parts." Another work in the collection, *Flower #1* (1993), shows the result of Baechler's surrogate figuration and his economical graphic sense.

Although his work veers more toward abstraction and he has spent large parts of his career outside the U.S. (mostly in France), painter James Brown was, for a time, part of the same New York scene as Basquiat, Haring and Baechler. His work of the early 1980s uses a raw, totemic figuration (influenced by Jean

Miguel Barceló, *Locus*,
1989

Dubuffet and African art) that has
affinities with Basquiat's work. But
running through Brown's oeuvre is a
strong religious feeling, one that
shows the influence of his Catholic
education. (He received his BFA from Immaculate Heart College in Hollywood.)
This aspect of his work is confirmed by an oil and zinc on panel painting titled
Stabat Mater Yellow VI (1989). The painting, which shows a pair of thin totemic
forms against a metallic gold ground, belongs to a large series of works inspired
by Giovanni Battista Pergolesi's famous 1736 musical setting of the Stabat Mater
Doloroso hymn, which offers compassion for the mother of Christ at the
Crucifixion. One commentator on Brown — French poet and critic Jean Frémon
— tells us that the title of the series is connected to the artist's habit of listening
to the same piece of music again and again as he works on a series of paintings. [3]

Other works in this collection give a sense of how widespread the revival of
figurative painting was in the 1980s. Mexican-American painter Ray Smith, who
began showing in the mid-1980s, combines allusions to European high-
modernism with vernacular Mexican imagery and the disjunctive visual syntax of
David Salle and Julian Schnabel. His large four-panel oil and wax on wood
painting *Erotica, Neurotica* (1989), uses motifs from Ferdinand Léger behind
sparring animals. In Europe, this figurative painting revival was first felt in
Germany and Italy but soon spread to other countries where, encountering
specific cultural traditions and conditions and the unique sensibilities of
individual artists, it took on a variety of forms. In Spain, the most prominent of
the new figurative painters was Miguel Barceló, an internationally known artist
who divides his time between Paris, the island of Mallorca (where he was born)
and the West African nation of Mali, whose Dogon culture has been a major
influence on his work since 1988. Cuisine is one of the recurring themes in
Barceló's highly tactile and densely composed paintings; books are another. Both
are present in the large, densely painted canvas *Soupe d'Ane* (1992). The French

Jean-Charles Blais, *Untitled*, 1984

title, which translates as "Donkey Soup," allows us to identify the legs sticking out of the huge oval cauldron that fills nearly all of this giant painting. Most of the other ingredients aren't so easy to identify, though onions, turnips and shellfish seem to be present. Most unusually, there appears to be an open book near the upper center of the painting. One can make out some upside down letters on its spine that spell out "*todo*," Spanish for "everything," which might well be the recipe for this dish. For Barceló, soup has metaphorical meaning. Speaking of paintings like *Soupe d'Ane*, he once said, "The soup represents a little bit the image of cultural chaos; it is the last image to create when nothing else is possible." [4] In such works, he says, he wants "to show painting for what it is, its wealth and its misery."

In France, a movement coalesced in 1981 around the banner of "Figuration Libre" (Free Figuration). The two Figuration Libre works in the collection, Robert Combas' painting *Autoportrait en cuiseur d'oeuf* (Self-Portrait as Egg Cooker) (1981) and Jean-Charles Blais' gouache *Untitled* (1984), suggest the scope of the movement, which included comic-book influenced artists such as Combas and more traditional Neo-Expressionist painters such as Blais. Complicating Blais' expressionist style, however, was his practice of appropriating images from other artists, mostly early 20th-century modernists, and pushing his work toward abstraction. Speaking in 1984, the year of this work, he said, "I paint figures which are no longer people but objects …. The body has become a piece of painting." [5] Combas' work, by contrast, is brashly populist, borrowing enthusiastically from comic books, art brut and hand-painted advertisements, stirring in sexuality, violence and satiric scenes of everyday life (as in *Autoportrait en cuiseur d'oeuf*). Stressing his working-class background, Combas says that in the beginning his style was "a derisive reaction against the intellectual painters of the 1970s." [6] It's important to keep in mind, however, that Combas' embrace of a comic-strip style of figuration reflects the relatively high esteem that the French

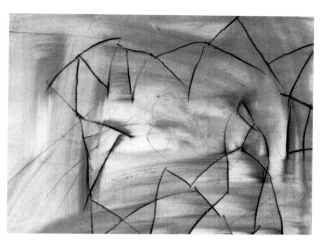

Daniel Dezeuze, *Untitled*, 1984

cartoonists or *bande dessinée* have long enjoyed in France.

Although Combas doesn't name names, I suspect that those "intellectual painters of the 1970s" included participants in the Supports/Surfaces movement. It is another mark of this collection's openness that it can accommodate Figuration Libre painters and two of the leading Supports/Surfaces artists: Daniel Dezeuze and Noël Dolla. Launched in the late 1960s, Supports/Surfaces focused on the components (physical and ideological) of abstraction. In parallel to Postminimalism in the U.S. and Arte Povera in Italy, Supports/Surfaces sought to break existing boundaries, whether through the use of unstretched canvas, outdoor exhibitions or Marxist analysis, while maintaining a strong retinal and tactile component and references to the modernist grid. Dezeuze, represented here by *Untitled* (1984), a chalk on paper drawing, is a multifaceted, often allusive artist. His best-known works include large, flexible wood lattices. Sometimes painted, sometimes not, they are exhibited both rolled and unrolled, existing somewhere between painting and sculpture. His work often touches on topology and oblique representation.

Dolla is even more varied than Dezeuze in his artistic practice. Since the late 1960s, he has continually sought out new approaches to painting, submitting the medium to his restless imagination and intellect. This has meant everything from abstractions created on handkerchiefs and dish towels, to three giant dots painted temporarily in the sand of a beach in Nice. In the mid-1980s, Dolla created the "Tchernobyl" series, which includes the three-panel painting illustrated in the catalogue. When these works, which feature primitive figures and roughly textured surfaces, were first shown in public, some accused Dolla, whose previous work had been exclusively abstract, of jumping on the Neo-Expressionist bandwagon. Only later did Dolla reveal that he had made the paintings with one eye covered and one hand (the one he normally favors) tied behind his back. The paintings were at once Dolla's critique of what he saw as the

Roland Flexner, *Untitled (cluster of skulls)*, 1993

regressive tendencies of Neo-Expressionism and his protest against the then-recent nuclear disaster in Chernobyl.

Another important figure in recent French art, Roland Flexner, is well represented in the Cottrell-Lovett collection. Born in Nice, Flexner has been living in New York for the last 20 years, where he has developed a unique body of work that combines meticulous execution and emotional power. A pair of large canvases from 1987 — *Untitled (people with torches)* and *Untitled (blue room with curving line)* — exemplify Flexner's approach to painting: instantly memorable images; a smooth, almost impersonal facture; compositions that stress the contours of the forms; and a certain withholding of meaning. Are these luminous torch wielders a threatening mob or a celebratory crowd? Is this schematic blue room an abstraction veering toward representation or vice versa? The paintings also show Flexner's penchant for technical experimentation. *Untitled (people with torches)* is gilded, which means the paint has been laid down over a tin surface, while *Untitled (blue room with curving line)* uses the gilding technique for the line of the title and oil and wax for the rest of this cool monochrome. The 1993 graphite drawing *Untitled (cluster of skulls)* belongs to a series of precisely rendered small-scale drawings, many of which utilize similar momento mori imagery. The "bubble drawings" are prime examples of Flexner's ongoing series of works made with soap and India ink bubbles, which the artist blows and then causes to burst onto sheets of paper. The range of effects in these unconventionally made, incredibly detailed drawings is amazing. They can evoke landscapes, swirling rivers, underground strata, celestial bodies or microscopic life forms. As I observed in an article on Flexner published last year in *Art in America*, the bubble drawings "offer miniature subtleties of shape and line that no human hand could ever achieve, and a degree of complexity that even computers might find unattainable. There's not a single pinprick-sized area of the drawings that doesn't offer something to look at." [7]

Dominique Figarella, *Untitled*, 1993

Also present in the collection are three of the best younger French artists: Dominique Figarella, Philippe Mayaux and Edouard Prulhière. In the work of Figarella, who was a student and assistant of Dolla's before launching his own career, the process of making the painting becomes inseparable from the final result. In an early work from 1993, the artist uses wide bandages to hold the pink and green paint in place. On the one hand the bandages encourage a metaphorical reading — painting is in a wounded state, the artist must heal it — and on the other, they establish a subtly warping grid and give the painting a simultaneous sense of thickness and transparency. In a more recent work, *Repaint?* (2002), the paint is contained by the rubber tips of five toilet plungers compressed underneath a sheet of clear Lexan®. As usual with Figarella, the work conveys a sense of formal tension and irreverent, do-it-yourself ingenuity. Prulhière, who lived in New York for a number of years but recently returned to France, takes a similarly irreverent stance toward painting. In *Waiting for the Elevator* (2003), several vividly colored canvases seem to have been taken off their stretchers and roughly reassembled to create a painting-sculpture hybrid that is at once violent and tender. Mayaux calls on a very different tradition: the mocking, visually paradoxical Surrealism of René Magritte, mixed with Marcel Duchamp's pun-laden erotics. A master of a faux-anonymous representational style, Mayaux often loads his paintings with outrageous sexual puns.

The collection also includes some of New York's strongest painters: Jonathan Lasker, Suzanne McClelland, Amy Sillman and Deborah Kass, each of whom has developed a wholly individual response to the achievements of mid 20th-century modernism. Lasker's bold, thought-inducing paintings, which are careful enlargements of small sketches, reinvent gesture as a decorative element and a philosophical conundrum. McClelland also finds new ways to work with gestural painting, using eccentrically formed letters as a kind of trellis for her densely layered, fanciful yet tough-minded abstractions. More lyrical than Lasker or McClelland, but also willing to follow her rich visual imagination into cartoony imagery, Sillman fruitfully explores the zone between figuration and abstraction that attracts so many of the artists in this collection. For her part, Kass takes a more critical view of the modernist heritage, juxtaposing classic images (Pablo Picasso's *Portrait of Gertrude Stein* and Jasper John's *The Critic Laughs*) and hijacking others' styles (her Warholian painting of Barbra Streisand) to perpetrate acts of cultural subversion, as well as make some gorgeous paintings.

British-born, New York-based Malcolm Morley is represented by two important paintings that combine nautical and aerial imagery. After doing pioneering work as a Photorealist and a Neo-Expressionist (avant la lettre), Morley began making paintings that feature exquisitely rendered ships and planes. Many of these works are closely connected to a traumatic childhood memory that the artist only recently recovered through psychoanalysis. Living in London during World War II, his family was several times forced to leave their homes by German bombing. In one instance, the young Morley had placed a recently completed, much-beloved model ship on a windowsill. That night the shock wave from a VI rocket attack dislodged and destroyed the balsa-wood model, a loss that became emblematic of all the dislocations Morley suffered as a youth. In these recent works, which feature many surprising details (such as the trompe l'oeil frame in *Santa Maria with Sopwith Camel Wing* 1996), Morley has transmuted this piece of autobiography into audacious, virtuosic paintings.

Another American-loving Brit, David Hockney, is represented by several early works, including *Untitled (Landscape #1 and #2)*, which, like Morley's *Santa Maria with Sopwith Camel Wing*, has a painted border — in this case, representing two window frames. The year this diptych was painted, 1964, was important for Hockney on at least two counts: he moved to Los Angeles (after a semester teaching at the University of Iowa) and switched from using oil to acrylic paint. As critic Marco Livingston points out, the matte surface of Hockney's acrylic work is related to the "flat, anonymous surfaces of photographs."[8] In his monograph on

O. Winston Link, *Above Hawks Bill Creek*, ca. 1956

Hockney, Livingston also tells us that in 1964 the artist acquired his first Polaroid camera. (Interestingly, the O. Winston Link train photographs from the 1950s in this collection have spatial anomalies not unlike some of Hockney's mid-1960s canvases.) Stylistically close to both Hockney's Iowa paintings and his first Los Angeles canvases, this diptych features a simplified mountainous landscape that one might surmise Hockney encountered while traveling from the Midwest to California.

The international flavor of this collection is echoed in one of the most recent additions to it: Barton Lidice Benes' *Souvenirs* (2003). A New York-based artist whose work frequently involves treating bits of pop-culture ephemera like holy relics, Benes operates in a self-invented aesthetic zone that overlaps with Joseph Cornell, the wunderkammer tradition and Andy Warhol's "time capsule" boxes. For *Souvenirs*, he used paper currency to fashion 72 tiny objects, each of which is representative of a different country: a wooden shoe for Holland, a steak for Argentina, what seems to be a detail of a Charles Rennie Macintosh window for Scotland, and so forth. Mounted as a grid in a box and individually labeled, these charms are miracles of craft and a witty commentary on the tyranny of national characteristics and the circulation of money. More somber is Benes' *Combination Therapy* (1993), a mosaic of a human skull made not from ceramic tiles but from AIDS drugs (specifically the pills used before the advent of the "cocktail"). Evoking a Mexican Dia de los Muertos celebration and once again displaying Benes' ingenuity, the piece is at once a rueful acknowledgement of death and a symbol of art's potential for triumph.

Endnotes

1. Richard Marshall, "Repelling Ghosts," *Jean-Michel Basquiat*, Whitney Museum of Art, New York, p. 15.
2. David Sheff, "Keith Haring: An Intimate Conversation," *Rolling Stone*, Aug. 10, 1989, p. 61.
3. Jean Frémon, "Le Sel de la Terre," *James Brown*, ed. Danilo Eccher, Galleria Civica di Arte Contemporanea, Trento, p. 128.
4. Jean-Louis Froment, "Romance," *Miguel Barceló*, Institute of Contemporary Art, Boston, 1986, p. 15.
5. Cited by Catherine Millet, *L'art contemporain en France*, Paris, Flammarion, 1994, p. 239.
6. See the Website www.combas.com.
7. Raphael Rubinstein, "When Bubbles Burst," *Art in America*, February 2003, pp. 96-99.
8. Marco Livingston, *David Hockney*, London, Thames and Hudson, 1996, p. 73.

COLOR PLATES

Donald Baechler, *Flower #1*, 1993

Donald Baechler, *Untitled*, 1988

Miguel Barceló, *In Vitro*, 1987

Miguel Barceló, *Soupe D'ane*, 1992

Jean-Michel Basquiat, *Three Delegates*, 1982

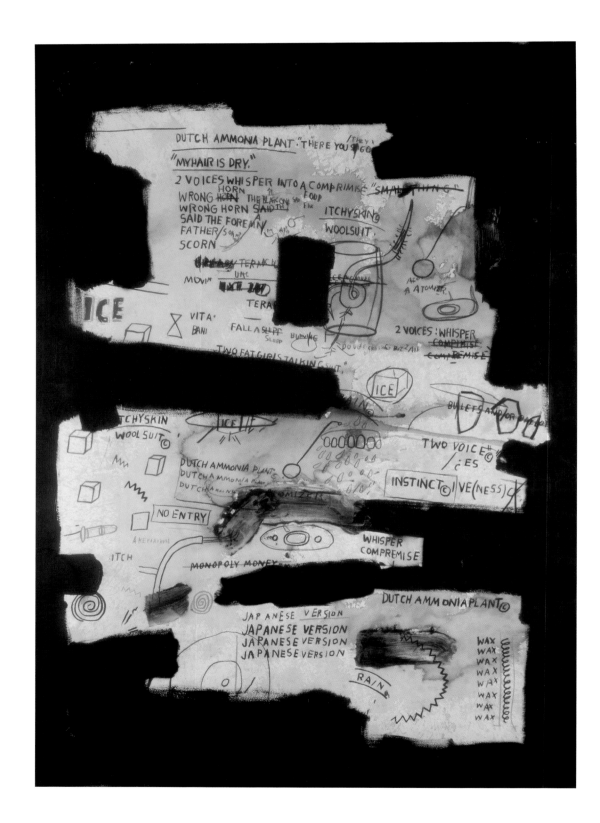

Jean-Michel Basquiat, *Untitled*, 1984

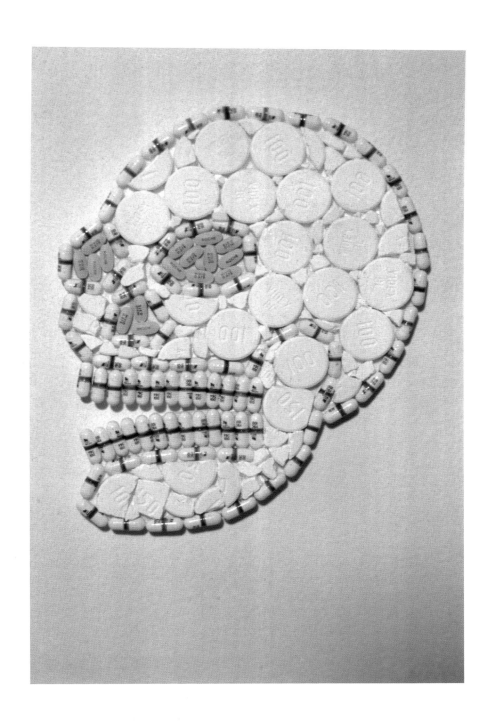

Barton Lidice Benes, *Combination Therapy*, 1993

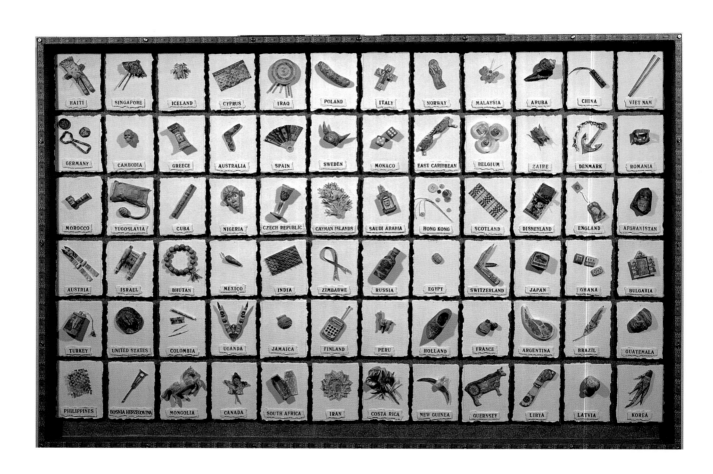

Barton Lidice Benes, *Souvenirs*, 2003

James Brown, *Stabat Mater Yellow VI*, 1989

Robert Combas, *Autoportrait en cuiseur d'oeuf*, 1984

Noël Dolla, *Tchernobyl*, 1986

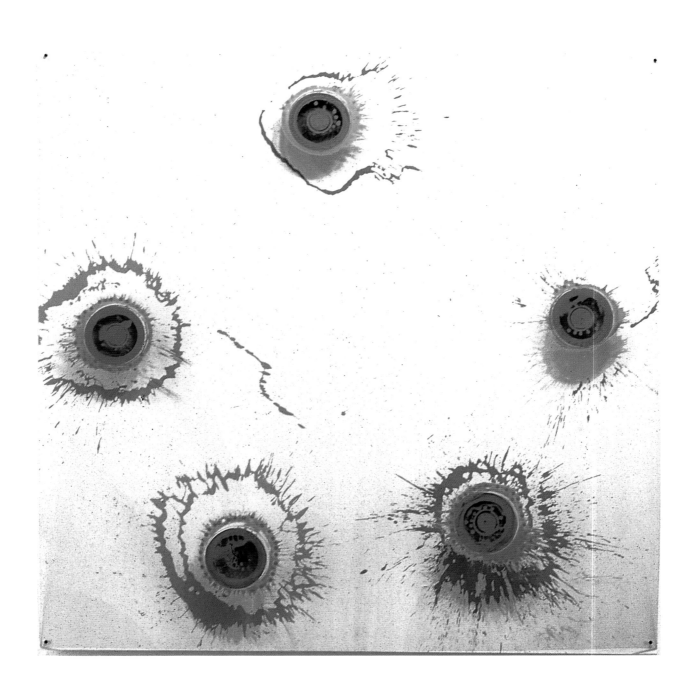

Dominique Figarella, *Repaint?*, 2000

Roland Flexner, *Untitled (blue room with curving line)*, 1987

Roland Flexner, *Untitled (people with torches)*, 1986

Keith Haring, *Untitled*, 1978

David Hockney, *Untitled (Landscape #1 and #2)*, 1964

Deborah Kass, *Call of the Wild (for Pat Steir)*, 1989

Deborah Kass, *How Do I Look?*, 1991

Jonathan Lasker, *Symbolic Farming*, 2001

Philippe Mayaux, *Arribo, Arribo*, 1997

Suzanne McClelland, *Wonder Woman and Diana*, 2000

Suzanne McClelland, *Purfuct*, 1996

Malcolm Morley, *Santa Maria with Sopwith Camel Wing*, 1996

Malcolm Morley, *Still Life with Two Planes*, 2001-2002

Edouard Prulhière, *Waiting for the Elevator*, 2003

Alexis Rockman, *Untitled*, 1992

Amy Sillman, *Monster*, 1996

Ray Smith, *Erotica, Neurotica*, 1989

CHECKLIST

Jean-Michel Alberola (French, b. Algeria, 1953)
L'Afrique, 1985
pastel on paper
42 1/2 x 29 in., each (set of 2)

Donald Baechler (American, b. 1956)
Untitled, 1988
acrylic, oil and collage on muslin
42 x 42 in.

Donald Baechler (American, b. 1956)
Untitled, 1990
bronze with dark patina
14 3/4 x 14 3/4 x 5 in.

Donald Baechler (American, b. 1956)
Flower #1, 1993
acrylic on canvas
91 x 61 in.

Donald Baechler (American, b. 1956)
Flower, 1995
ink, gesso, acrylic and collage on paper
16 3/4 x 14 in.

Miguel Barceló (Spanish, b. 1957)
Soupe d'Ane, 1992
mixed media on canvas
92 1/2 x 147 5/8 in.

Miguel Barceló (Spanish, b. 1957)
In Vitro, 1987
oil on canvas
90 1/2 x 118 1/4 in.

Miguel Barceló (Spanish, b. 1957)
Radis Coupe, 1988
gouache on paper
19 1/2 x 27 1/2 in.

Miguel Barceló (Spanish, b. 1957)
Locus, 1989
mixed media on canvas
78 3/4 x 118 3/4 in.

Jean-Michel Basquiat (American, 1960–1988)
Claudio, n.d.
crayon on paper
17 x 14 in.

Jean-Michel Basquiat (American, 1960–1988)
Three Delegates, 1982
acrylic, oil stick, collage on canvas
60 x 60 in.

Jean-Michel Basquiat (American, 1960–1988)
Untitled, 1984
oil and oil stick on paper
41 1/2 x 29 1/2 in.

Barton Lidice Benes (American, b. 1942)
Palette, 1990
mixed media on paper
28 x 20 in.

Barton Lidice Benes (American, b. 1942)
Laundered Money, 1990
mixed media construction
26 3/4 x 19 3/4 in.

Barton Lidice Benes (American, b. 1942)
Poison Dart, 1991
mixed media on paper
14 x 12 1/2 in.

Barton Lidice Benes (American, b. 1942)
Nest Egg, 1991
mixed media on paper
14 x 13 in.

Barton Lidice Benes (American, b. 1942)
Combination Therapy, 1993
mixed media on paper
13 x 11 in.

Barton Lidice Benes (American, b. 1942)
The Cremated Remains of Brenda, 1993
mixed media on paper
8 1/4 x 5 3/4 in.

Barton Lidice Benes (American, b. 1942)
Talisman, 1994
mixed media on paper
14 x 13 in.

Barton Lidice Benes (American, b. 1942)
Untitled, 1997
polychrome terracotta
11 x 9 1/4 x 3 in.

Barton Lidice Benes (American, b. 1942)
Basquiat Paintbrush, 2002
mixed media construction
14 x 11 x 3/4 in.

Barton Lidice Benes (American, b. 1942)
Candy Box, 2002
mixed media on paper
13 1/2 x 12 in.

Barton Lidice Benes (American, b. 1942)
Candy Box, 2003
mixed media construction
1 1/2 x 9 1/2 x 4 in.

Barton Lidice Benes (American, b. 1942)
Souvenirs, 2003
mixed media on paper mounted to board
72 1/4 x 48 x 3 1/4 in.

Jean-Charles Blais (French, b. 1956)
Untitled, 1984
gouache on paper
24 1/2 x 28 1/2 in.

Robert Brady (American, b. 1946)
Fall #3, 2002
wood, stone, string, paper
57 x 14 x 12 in.

James Brown (American, b. 1951)
Stabat Mater Yellow VI, 1989
oil and zinc on wood
61 5/8 x 75 1/4 x 2 in.

James Brown (American, b. 1951)
Untitled (New York), 1991
acrylic and gold leaf on panel
18 x 14 x 1 in.

Robert Combas (French, b. 1957)
Autoportrait en cuiseur d'oeuf, 1984
acrylic on canvas
67 x 79 in.

Robert Combas (French, b. 1957)
Fantasy Figures, 1995
acrylic on plaster; edition 2/8
21 5/8 x 14 x 9 in.

Robert Combas (French, b. 1957)
The Scarecrow, 1995
acrylic on plaster; edition 5/8
33 1/2 x 19 x 12 in.

Roy Dean De Forest (American, b. 1930)
Untitled, 1978
mixed media on paper
22 1/4 x 30 in.

Daniel Dezeuze (French, b. 1942)
Untitled, 1984
chalk on paper
22 1/4 x 30 in.

Daniel Dezeuze (French, b. 1942)
Untitled, 1991
acrylic on veneer glued on cardboard
10 3/4 x 10 x 1/4 in., each (set of 5)

Noël Dolla (French, b. 1945)
Tchernobyl, 1986
acrylic and gauze on wood
81 x 41 in., each (3 panels)

Noël Dolla (French, b. 1945)
Untitled #11, 1988
oil on wood
95 3/4 x 8 5/8 x 2 7/8 in.

Noël Dolla (French, b. 1945)
The Boat People #1, 1989
acrylic on wood with three feathers
8 3/4 x 31 1/2 x 2 1/2 in.

Noël Dolla (French, b. 1945)
Two Flags, 1991
collage and acrylic on wood
19 3/4 x 19 3/4 x 3/4 in.

Susan Etkin (American, b. 1955)
Untitled (Dryclean Series), 1990-1991
mixed media on paper
19 3/4 x 13 3/4 in.

Dominique Figarella (French, b. 1966)
Summer, 1993
acrylic on wood
10 1/4 x 9 1/2 in.

Dominique Figarella (French, b. 1966)
Untitled, 1993
acrylic and tricoplast bandages on wood
29 1/2 x 29 1/2 in.

Dominique Figarella (French, b. 1966)
Cut?, 2000
Lexan®, acrylic on Baltic birch, bandages
and vinyl plastic
60 x 60 x 6 in.

Dominique Figarella (French, b. 1966)
Repaint?, 2000
Lexan®, plungers, acrylic, oil on Baltic
birch
60 x 60 x 5 in.

Roland Flexner (French, b. 1944)
Untitled (four Camel boxes), 1971-1974
mixed media
9 1/4 x 4 7/8 x 1 1/2 in., each (set of 4)

Roland Flexner (French, b. 1944)
Untitled (man with cross), 1995
graphite on paper
14 x 11 in.

Roland Flexner (French, b. 1944)
Untitled (standing figure throwing light), 1985
oil and gilding on canvas
80 x 68 in.

Roland Flexner (French, b. 1944)
Untitled (people with torches), 1986
oil and gilding on canvas
48 x 72 in.

Roland Flexner (French, b. 1944)
Untitled (blue room with curving line), 1987
oil and gilding on canvas
48 x 72 in.

Roland Flexner (French, b. 1944)
Untitled (camel), 1991
graphite on paper
14 x 11 in.

Roland Flexner (French, b. 1944)
Untitled (cluster of skulls), 1993
graphite on paper
14 x 11 in.

Roland Flexner (French, b. 1944)
Untitled (bubble drawing, FP44), 2001
ink on paper
5 1/2 x 7 in.

Roland Flexner (French, b. 1944)
Untitled (bubble drawing, FP13), 2002
ink on paper
6 3/4 x 5 1/2 in.

Roland Flexner (French, b. 1944)
Untitled (bubble drawing, FP17), 2002
ink on paper
5 1/2 x 7 in.

Roland Flexner (French, b. 1944)
Untitled (bubble drawing, FP46), 2002
ink on paper
7 x 5 1/2 in.

Keith Haring (American, 1958–1990)
Untitled, 1978
oil on paper
102 x 33 in.

Keith Haring (American, 1958–1990)
Untitled, 1988
gouache and sumi ink on paper
60 x 40 in.

David Hockney (British, b. 1937)
Judy Blume, 1961
charcoal on paper
36 x 24 in.

David Hockney (British, b. 1937)
Mirror, Mirror on the Wall, Who is the Fairest of Them All, 1961
lithograph on paper
15 1/2 x 19 1/2 in.

David Hockney (British, b. 1937)
My Bonnie Lies Over the Sea, 1961
etching and aquatint on paper
17 3/4 x 17 3/4 in.

David Hockney (British, b. 1937)
Still Life, 1961
lithograph on paper
30 x 22 in.

David Hockney (British, b. 1937)
Kaisarion and All His Beauty, 1961
etching and aquatint on paper
19 1/4 x 10 3/4 in.

David Hockney (British, b. 1937)
Aggresive Head, 1961-1962
charcoal on paper
11 x 8 1/2 in.

David Hockney (British, b. 1937)
Figure "4-D," 1961-1962
charcoal and ink on paper
9 x 6 in.

David Hockney (British, b. 1937)
Study for "Cecchino Bracci, In Memoriam," 1962
ink on paper
11 x 8 1/2 in.

David Hockney (British, b. 1937)
In Memoriam, Cecchino Bracci, n.d.
ink on paper
10 x 14 1/4 in.

David Hockney (British, b. 1937)
Untitled, n.d.
ink on paper
9 x 6 in.

David Hockney (British, b. 1937)
XXV.XII.MCMLXI, n.d.
ink on paper
9 x 6 in.

David Hockney (British, b. 1937)
Untitled, n.d.
ink on paper
9 x 6 in.

David Hockney (British, b. 1937)
Untitled, n.d.
ink on paper
11 x 8 1/2 in.

David Hockney (British, b. 1937)
Untitled, n.d.
ink on paper
8 7/8 x 6 in.

David Hockney (British, b. 1937)
Untitled, n.d.
ink on paper
9 1/4 x 6 1/4 in.

David Hockney (British, b. 1937)
Untitled, n.d.
graphite on paper
9 x 6 in.

David Hockney (British, b. 1937)
Untitled, n.d.
ink on paper
9 x 6 in.

David Hockney (British, b. 1937)
Untitled (Landscape #1 and #2), 1964
acrylic on canvas (diptych)
24 x 24 in.

David Hockney (British, b. 1937)
Jungle Fever, 1964
lithograph on paper; edition AP
19 3/4 x 24 in.

Deborah Kass (American, b. 1952)
Call of the Wild (for Pat Steir), 1989
oil, enamel and acrylic on canvas
39 1/4 x 81 1/4 in.

Deborah Kass (American, b. 1952)
Short Stories, 1989
oil and enamel on canvas
32 1/4 x 65 1/4 in.

Deborah Kass (American, b. 1952)
How Do I Look?, 1991
oil on canvas
50 x 100 in.

Deborah Kass (American, b. 1952)
Gold Barbra (The Jewish Jackie Series), 1992
silkscreen, ink and acrylic on canvas
30 x 24 in.

Deborah Kass (American, b. 1952)
Making Men #4, 1992-1994
oil, enamel and acrylic on canvas
78 x 60 in.

Jonathan Lasker (American, b. 1948)
Untitled, 1990
crayon on paper
22 x 30 in.

Jonathan Lasker (American, b. 1948)
Improved Expressions, 1991
oil on linen
72 x 54 in.

Jonathan Lasker (American, b. 1948)
Symbolic Farming, 2001
oil on linen
60 x 80 in.

O. Winston Link (American, 1914-2000)
Poolside, ca. 1955
black and white photograph
16 x 20 in.

O. Winston Link (American, 1914-2000)
At the Drive-In, ca. 1955
black and white photograph
16 x 20 in.

O. Winston Link (American, 1914-2000)
Above Hawks Bill Creek, ca. 1956
black and white photograph
20 x 16 in.

Robert Longo (American, b. 1953)
Untitled, 1983
oil on paper
26 1/2 x 27 in.

Robert Mapplethorpe
(American, 1946-1989)
Untitled #3 Green Nude with Apple, 1985
three color photogravure; edition 22/60
30 x 24 3/4 in.

Robert Mapplethorpe
(American, 1946-1989)
Irises, 1987
photogravure; edition PP
34 x 32 1/8 in.

Philippe Mayaux (French, b. 1961)
Genius, 1990-1991
acrylic, oil and brass on wood
13 x 17 x 5 in., each (set of 3)

Philippe Mayaux (French, b. 1961)
Laisse ici toutes (les esperances), 1992
oil on canvas
12 x 12 in.

Philippe Mayaux (French, b. 1961)
Quand au monstre humide de Veronique,
1992-1993
oil on canvas on metal towel rack
13 x 22 in.

Philippe Mayaux (French, b. 1961)
Arribo, Arribo, 1997
oil on canvas
10 3/4 x 8 3/4 in.

Suzanne McClelland (American, b. 1959)
Always, 1992
acrylic, charcoal, gesso and clay on canvas
72 x 72 in.

Suzanne McClelland (American, b. 1959)
Someday, 1992
acrylic, pigment and gesso on canvas
72 x 72 in.

Suzanne McClelland (American, b. 1959)
91295d, 1995
clay, gesso, synthetic media, acrylic, enamel
and dry pigment on canvas
96 x 26 in.

Suzanne McClelland (American, b. 1959)
Purfuct, 1996
charcoal, synthetic medium, acrylic, gesso,
dry pigment and enamel on canvas
68 x 72 in.

Suzanne McClelland (American, b. 1959)
tips #3 (between the lines), 1997-1999
gouache, absorbent ground, conte, ink,
acrylic, pastel and charcoal on paper
107 1/2 x 80 in.

Suzanne McClelland (American, b. 1959)
Wonder Woman and Diana, 2000
absorbant ground, polymer emulsion and
acrylic on buried canvas
28 x 30 in.

Mark Mennin (American, b. 1960)
Hidden Sound, 1995
marble
38 x 7 x 11 1/2 in.

Malcolm Morley (British, b. 1931)
Untitled, n.d.
watercolor on paper
12 x 16 in.

Malcolm Morley (British, b. 1931)
*A Hun Burst Into Flames and Another Came
Spinning Earthward*, 1992
watercolor on paper
21 1/2 x 30 1/8 in.

Malcolm Morley (British, b. 1931)
Santa Maria with Sopwith Camel Wing, 1996
oil on linen
56 x 72 in.

Malcolm Morley (British, b. 1931)
Still Life with Two Planes, 2001-2002
oil on linen with watercolor and encaustic
and plaster attachments
36 x 28 1/8 x 4 1/2 in.

Todd Murphy (American, b. 1962)
Untitled (Two Figures), 1994
Kaoline, tar emulsion and oilstick on paper
33 x 30 in.

Brigitte Nahon (French, b. 1960)
Untitled, 1994
graphite on paper
30 x 22 in.

Manuel Neri (American, b. 1930)
Seated Female Figure, 1961
plaster, wood, wire and burlap
28 x 48 x 38 in.

Edouard Prulhière (French, b. 1965)
Untitled, 1993
oil and acrylic on canvas
74 x 70 in.

Edouard Prulhière (French, b. 1965)
Waiting for the Elevator, 2003
mixed media
77 x 36 x 12 in.

Archie Rand (American, b. 1949)
Den Barley, 1994
acrylic and mixed media on canvas
16 x 20 in.

Alexis Rockman (American, b. 1962)
Untitled, 1992
ink and watercolor on paper
14 1/8 x 20 in.

Andres Serrano (American, b. 1953)
Crucifixion, 1987
Cibachrome print on glass
27 1/2 x 40 in.

Amy Sillman (American, b. 1955)
Monster, 1996
gouache on paper
30 x 22 1/2 in.

Ray Smith (American, b. 1959)
Mariana, 1982
wood and steel
47 x 10 3/4 x 10 3/4 in.

Ray Smith (American, b. 1959)
Untitled I, 1989
monocut on paper
30 x 22 in.

Ray Smith (American, b. 1959)
Erotica, Neurotica, 1989
oil and wax on wood
84 x 144 in.

Ray Smith (American, b. 1959)
Biker, 1990
oil on paper
25 x 30 in.

Gregory Thompson
(American, 1952-1989)
Max, ca. 1980-1981
oil on canvas
40 1/4 x 28 3/4 in.

John Francis Tirado (American, b. 1969)
Untitled, 1993
mixed media on panel
21 x 13 7/8 in.

Makhi Xenakis (French, b. 1956)
Untitled, 1994
mixed media on paper
25 x 17 in.

Makhi Xenakis (French, b. 1956)
Untitled, 1995
mixed media on paper
25 1/2 x 19 1/2 in.

Makhi Xenakis (French, b. 1956)
Untitled, 2002
mixed media on paper, fake fur
13 x 11 1/2 x 1 1/2 in.

CREDITS

The Orlando Museum of Art would like to thank an anonymous donor for generously supporting this exhibition.

This catalogue was designed and produced on a G4 MacIntosh computer by Meredy Jenkins, Orlando, Florida, and edited by Michelle Ghorbanian, Orlando, Florida. Two thousand copies of the catalogue were printed five-color process plus aqueous coating, direct to plate on 100# Corniche Velvet Text and Cover papers by Fidelity Press, Orlando, Florida.

Photography Credits:

Donald Baechler, Courtesy of Cheim & Reed Gallery and the artist

Jean-Michel Basquiat, © 2004 Artists Rights Society (ARS), New York/ ADAGP, Paris

O. Winston Link, © O. Winston Link Estate. Courtesy Robert Mann Gallery

Jorge Queiroz, Courtesy of Galerie Nathalie Obadia and the artist

Alexis Rockman, © 1992 Alexis Rockman. Courtesy Gorney Bravin + Lee

Raymond Martinot, New Smyrna Beach, Florida, photographed the following works for the catalogue:

> Barton Lidice Benes, *Souvenirs*, 2003
>
> Nöel Dolla, *Tchernobyl*, 1986
>
> Dominique Figarella, *Untitled*, 1993
>
> David Hockney, *In Memoriam, Cecchino Bracci*, n.d.
>
> Deborah Kass, *Call of the Wild (for Pat Steir)*, 1989
>
> O. Winston Link, *Above Hawks Bill Creek*, ca. 1956
>
> O. Winston Link, *At the Drive-In*, ca. 1955
>
> Philippe Mayaux, *Arribo, Arribo*, 1995
>
> Todd Murphy, *Untitled (Two Figures)*, 1994
>
> Manuel Neri, *Seated Female Figure*, 1961
>
> Amy Sillman, *Monster*, 1996

Sue Scott, New York, New York, photographed Malcolm Morley and James Cottrell for the catalogue

Dan Eifert, New York, New York, photographed the images for the front and back cover

Back Cover: Donald Baechler, fountain commission, residence of James Cottrell and Joseph Lovett